PENNINE STEAM

Fowler LMS 'Patriot' class three-cylinder 4-6-0 No 45520 *Llandudno* is the epitome of Pennine Steam as it storms through Slaithwaite station on the climb to Standedge Tunnel with a Sunday York-Manchester express in the 1950s.

PENNINE STEAM

Kenneth Field & Brian Stephenson

LONDON

IAN ALLAN LTD

To Mark and Michelle who know
Steam and Simon who will.

First published 1977

ISBN 0 7110 0793 4

Published by Ian Allan Ltd, Shepperton, Surrey,
and printed in the United Kingdom by
Ian Allan Printing Ltd.

Introduction

The volcanic, tertiary and ice ages which threw up and ground down my home area of England known as the Pennines, provided for many of man's future needs in the shape of lead, zinc, coal, ironstone, limestone, millstone, granite to build and road metal, quartz, barites, etc. Stretching from Derby to Penrith and forming the backbone of England, the area bred a hardy race of people and way of living. Lack of knowledge and use for the materials, and of a means of transport, meant very slow exploitation of the mineral riches. Despite Roman engineers and road building it was not until the late 1700s that improved methods of transport by river, road and canal stimulated the winning of certain minerals in greater quantity.

Throughout this period artists sought to illustrate the way of life and transport of their time. With the coming of expansive steam power after water and wind power, they had the chance to portray the rapidly growing momentum of industry. Coal and lime were the principal everyday ingredients. The birth of tramways in the late 1700s was followed in the early 1800s by steam locomotion in Leeds and Durham at a time when fodder was expensive, encouraging the replacement of horses. The influx of Geordie and Leeds engineers with little pre-knowledge of construction methods soon saw, throughout the Pennines, the rapid levelling of mountain and vale for the steam railway.

Once again artists set out to protray for posterity the scenes they saw as King Steam invaded every nook and cranny of the land. Fox Talbot's disciples developed the new method of using reflected light to emboss chemically-treated glass plates, and thus another new industry was born using rare metals. It developed faster as the pace of railway building slowed. By the late 1800s it was possible to photograph a train at speed, so that by 1910 any man could with minimal training be his own artist, with little chance of failure.

Ever since then and up to the present time, a never-ending variety of glass-eyed cameras with as varied an assortment of users has been vying to produce the best picture of their favourite beast, the steam locomotive. My own efforts stem from a lifetime's interest in all things mechanical, and from living with or near steam-motivated machinery, plus a late desire to capture a small part of it for future reflection. Thinking in motorway terms, it has barely taken an instant for steam locomotion to die; yet the world is by many thought richer

5

for its demise, as it leaves for better use the principal mineral — coal — which was its energy and reason for its birth.

A way of life has come and gone, relatively in a flash. We shall never see its like again, so any illustration of it is better than none. It is my belief that no camera has bettered the efforts of Bourne and Tait, though they improved on Turner. Within the last 80 years a remarkable succession of superb photographs of all aspects of the railway scene has appeared; many from the early 1900s are the equal of today. Brought up among the sounds and smells of 'Georges', 'Duffs', 'Fat Marias', 'Princes', 'Claughtons', 'Baby Scots', and later the ubiquitous Class Five and all things Gresley, I like many others thought they would last forever. However, irreversible events overtook King Steam. While it is still possible to photograph steam locomotives in action the full atmosphere, to me, has vanished forever.

There can be very few of man's creations so well documented, illustrated and sung about. Personal, unphotographed reflections on stations like Leeds and York provoke memories of shining 'Hunts' and 'Shires', and of double-headed 2Ps and Compounds before the 'Jubilees' came in. Leeds produced its own atmosphere and a smell found nowhere else in the area, due to the city's large variety of locomotives and stock, the different lubricating oils and coal they used, meals cooking in the variety of restaurant cars that passed through, and the all-pervading North Eastern oil gas. Somewhere there was always a donkey pump panting in the background and whistle tones galore. Smokebox sounds gave away many an unseen locomotive's origin, especially at night, and this applied on all lines in the area. From the hefty beat of a Robinson 'Tiny' banked in the rear and blasting up through Penistone with coal from Wath, the contented 'wuffle' of a 'Crimson Rambler' cruising through Walton en-route to Sheffield, the six-to-a-bar beat of a Gresley three-cylinder engine on Beeston bank (possibly a rhubarb special for Kings Cross Goods) or a Wessie 'Super D' anywhere on freight or passenger — all were vocally unmistakable. Manchester Victoria/Exchange, at the other end of my personal route, could not muster up as much variety, but it generated plenty of atmosphere, especially in Wakes Week.

6

Lacking seven league boots my efforts at photography by no means circumscribe the Pennines and are confined to the last years of steam on the routes traversed. It is with grateful thanks that I commend Brian Stephenson's efforts to produce from my negatives worthwhile results. He has also contributed some of his own photographs and has designed the layout. Nothing is produced without some help, and my wife often remarks that 'if I'd a pound for every hour spent by or on some railway I'd be rich'. Without the efforts of Pete Sunderland and his flying machine, many pictures would never have been. So, to Dot, Pete and Brian go my special thanks in seeing a book produced; and to the publishers, with whom I've had a long-distance affinity — thank you! I trust the result will please all who peruse and remember with me.

A plume of steam
O'er hill, through dale,
A whistle's strident call,
Now gone beyond recall.

Yet here again
With unveiled eye
The scene we thought 'the most',
As once again, in memory lane,
We meet a friendly ghost.

Golcar,   Kenneth Field
May 1976

Stanier LMS Class 8F
2-8-0 No 48098 pounds
towards Whatstandwell
before commencing the
climb to Peak Forest at
Rowsley with a heavy
iron-ore train bound for
Lancashire Steel at Irlam
on a freezing February 12,
1966.

ABOVE: A Derby-Manchester stopping train draws into Bakewell on the now closed section of the Midland route over the Peak, hauled by Fowler MR Class 4F 0-6-0 No 43985, on June 4, 1960.

UPPER LEFT: Rebuilt Johnson MR Class 3F 0-6-0 No 43496 runs light through Bakewell as LMS Class 4F 0-6-0 No 44538 banks an iron-ore train headed by a pair of 8F 2-8-0s on June 4, 1960. Heavy freight trains over the Peak were normally banked from Rowsley to Peak Forest.

LOWER LEFT: Another picture taken on June 4, 1960 showing Class 8F 2-8-0 No 48716 hurrying downhill through Bakewell station with a southbound freight.

UPPER LEFT: Hughes/Fowler LMS 'Crab' 2-6-0 No 42942 leaves Headstone Tunnel and crosses Monsal Dale Viaduct with a down coal train.

LOWER LEFT: Heading home to
Rowsley, Class 4F 0-6-0
No 44046 runs light downhill
between Litton and Cressbrook
Tunnels on July 19, 1963.

ABOVE: BR standard Class 9F
2-10-0 No 92049 heads an up
freight in the short gap between
Litton and Cressbrook Tunnels on
July 19, 1963.

Stanier LMS Class 5 4-6-0
No 45188 passes through
Millers Dale station with a
southbound express freight on
May 21, 1966. A diesel train for
Buxton can just been seen
waiting to depart in the platform
on the far left.

ABOVE: A coal train for Buxton leaves Ashwood Dale Tunnel on the branch from Millers Dale behind 'Crab' 2-6-0 No 42942, May 16, 1959.

UPPER LEFT: Class 8F 2-8-0 No 48254 eases past the limestone workings at Peak Forest after the climb from Dove Holes Tunnel with empty ICI limestone hoppers from Northwich for the works at Tunstead.

LOWER LEFT: A stranger at Millers Dale, rebuilt Robinson GCR Class O4/8 2-8-0 No 63788 passes through with a northbound freight on June 4, 1960.

UPPER LEFT: Stanier LMS
'Jubilee' class 4-6-0 No 45593
Kolhapur drifts down from
Cowburn Tunnel towards the site
of Chinley East Junction with a
special from Leeds on April 22,
1967.

ABOVE: A Stanier 'Black Five'
climbs round the curve from
Chapel-en-le-Frith to Dove Holes
Tunnel with an evening
Manchester Central-Derby train
on June 27, 1959. Cowburn
Tunnel on the Hope Valley line
cuts through the hills in the
background.

LEFT: A Saturday evening
engineers train comes round the
curve from Chapel-en-le-Frith
behind Stanier LMS Class 5
2-6-0 No 42947 on September
18, 1965.

RIGHT: Class 4F 0-6-0
No 44265 shunts the yard at
Peak Forest on June 4, 1960.

ABOVE: Thompson LNER Class B1 4-6-0 No 61093 approaches Hope with the 4.31pm Sheffield Midland-Chinley train on July 20, 1963. The use of B1 4-6-0s on Hope Valley trains was commonplace after the Eastern Region took control of the former LMS lines in the Sheffield area.

UPPER RIGHT: Riddles 'Austerity' Class WD 2-8-0 No 90190 rounds the curve from Chinley North to Chinley East Junctions and heads for Cowburn Tunnel and the Hope Valley line with a train of coal empties.

LOWER RIGHT: With Cracken Edge high above, Class 8F 2-8-0 No 48759 clanks downhill towards Chinley station with a down freight on September 18, 1965.

LEFT: Rebuilt Johnson Class 3F 0-6-0 No 43558 passes Hagues Bar on the New Mills-Marple line with a westbound freight.

TOP: BR standard 'Britannia' class Pacific No 70014 *Iron Duke* hurries past New Mills South Junction with the up 'Palatine' from Manchester Central to St Pancras on June 27, 1959.

ABOVE: A Tunstead-Northwich ICI limestone train approaches New Mills South Junction behind Class 8F 2-8-0 No 48135 on June 27, 1959.

ABOVE: An up freight leaves the southern end of Disley Tunnel at Disley behind Class 4F 0-6-0 No 44134 on July 4, 1959.

UPPER RIGHT: Robinson GCR Class J10/6 0-6-0 No 65194 leaves the other end of Disley Tunnel at Hazel Grove with a freight for the CLC on August 30, 1958.

RIGHT: 'Crab' 2-6-0 No 42818, fitted with Reidinger rotary poppet valve gear, climbs the 1 in 100 from Hazel Grove to Disley Tunnel with a freight for Gow Hole Sidings on August 30, 1958.

UPPER LEFT: Robinson GCR Class A5 4-6-2T No 69817 draws to a halt at Bredbury with a Saturday evening local from Macclesfield to Manchester London Road.

LOWER LEFT: A Saturday Manchester London Road-Macclesfield train enters Romiley station behind Thompson Class L1 2-6-4T No 67781.

ABOVE: Stanier LMS Class 3 2-6-2T No 40124 arrives at Heaton Mersey with a Manchester Central-Stockport Teviot Dale local.

RIGHT: 'Britannia' Pacific No 70032 Tennyson pulls away from Stockport on the last leg of its journey with a Euston-Manchester London Road via Stoke express.

ABOVE: Stanier LMS 'Princess Royal' class four-cylinder Pacific No 46210 *Lady Patricia* winds its way into Manchester London Road station with an express from Euston.

UPPER LEFT: 'Britannia' Pacific No 70044, fitted with two Westinghouse brake pumps for trials with express freight trains, backs out of Manchester London Road with the stock of its express from Euston.

LOWER LEFT: An Ordsall Lane-Longsight transfer freight drifts through the MSJ&A platforms at Manchester London Road behind Class 8F 2-8-0 No 48680.

ABOVE: Robinson Class A5 4-6-2T No 69823 departs from Manchester London Road with a Macclesfield via Romiley local.

LEFT: A Manchester London Road-Guide Bridge-Oldham local is seen on arrival at Oldham Clegg Street behind Robinson GCR Class C13 4-4-2T No 67421.

UPPER RIGHT: Class O4/8 2-8-0 No 63841 passes Ashton Junction and enters Guide Bridge station with a freight for Ardwick at Whitsun 1957.

LOWER RIGHT: Stanier LMS Class 4 2-6-4T No 42560 arrives at Guide Bridge with the Liverpool Central-Harwich boat train. Here the 2-6-4T will be changed for an electric engine for the run to Sheffield over Woodhead.

UPPER RIGHT: Gresley LNER Class O2 three-cylinder 2-8-0 No 63972 leaves one of the two sulphurous single bores of the old Woodhead Tunnel at Dunford Bridge with a through freight from Manchester to the south.

LOWER RIGHT: After a long wait in the sidings Robinson GCR Class O4 2-8-0 No 63683 gets the road through Dunford Bridge station and into the Woodhead Tunnel with a westbound freight for the Manchester area.

BELOW: Thompson Class B1 4-6-0 No 61228 about to leave Dunford Bridge and enter the Woodhead Tunnel with a Sheffield Victoria-Manchester London Road limited-stop service shortly before electric traction took over through the new tunnel in September 1954. It carries the 'South Yorkshireman' headboard reversed on the buffer beam.

LEFT: Stanier Black Five 4-6-0 No 45333 hurtles through Dunford Bridge with a lightweight Manchester-Leicester football special while in the distance a heavy freight is banked up to the Woodhead Tunnel.

RIGHT: A Marylebone-Manchester London Road express nears Hazelhead on the climb to Dunford Bridge behind Class B1 4-6-0 No 61155.

BELOW: Gresley LNER Class K3 three-cylinder 2-6-0 No 61896 passes Penistone Goods signalbox with a Saturday Yarmouth-Manchester holiday train.

ABOVE: Robinson GCR 'Improved Director' Class D11 4-4-0 No 62667 *Somme* and a Class N5 0-6-2T are caught in the evening light after arrival at Penistone with a train from Doncaster via Mexborough. The N5 pilot was attached at Barnsley for the climb to Penistone.

RIGHT: A rare occasion at Penistone with both the north and southbound 'North Country Continentals' in the station. Class B1 4-6-0 No 61192 is on the Liverpool-Harwich train. Above the engine can be seen the LYR branch to Huddersfield curving away over the viaduct.

BELOW: Gresley Class A3 three-cylinder Pacific No 60104 *Solario* gets to grips with the curving uphill start from Penistone with the morning Marylebone-Manchester London Road express.

BELOW RIGHT: BR standard Class 2MT 2-6-2T No 84013 pulls into Penistone off the LYR viaduct with a Bradford-Penistone train in June 1957. The second coach is on the pier which collapsed in World War I, precipitating an LYR tank into the River Don below.

LEFT: Class K3 2-6-0 No 61964 waits to take over a Manchester-Doncaster train at Sheffield Victoria on June 4, 1960.

BELOW: Gresley Class B17 three-cylinder 4-6-0 No 61627 *Aske Hall* waits in a bay at Sheffield Victoria after working in with the Harwich-Liverpool boat train.

UPPER RIGHT: Robinson Class D11 4-4-0 No 62670 *Marne* pulls out onto the Wicker Arch at Sheffield Victoria with empty stock as one of Sheffield's modern trams loads up for Lane Top in the street below.

LOWER RIGHT: On a cold January day Class B1 4-6-0 crosses the Wicker Arch as it leaves Sheffield Victoria with a stopping train for Manchester, passing a new Class EM2 electric locomotive.

LEFT: Ivatt Class 2 2-6-0 No 46500 rumbles over the girder bridge high above Barnsley's celebrated open market into Barnsley Court House station with a train from Sheffield Midland via Chapeltown. Both Court House station and the market are now gone.

BELOW LEFT: A Barnsley Court House-Sheffield via Chapeltown local nears Oaks Junction, Barnsley behind Ivatt Class 2 2-6-0 No 46502. This service still runs to Barnsley Exchange station.

BELOW: Ivatt Class 2 2-6-2T No 41326 prepares to leave Barnsley Court House with a push-pull train to Cudworth.

BOTTOM: Class O4/8 2-8-0 No 63726 pulls through Barnsley Exchange with a coal train for Manchester via Penistone.

UPPER LEFT: A Fowler LMS Class 4 2-6-4T runs bunker first over Lockwood Viaduct with an evening Penistone-Bradford train.

LOWER LEFT: A Bradford-Penistone train climbs Thurstonland Bank to Stocksmoor on the branch from Huddersfield hauled by Fairburn Class 4 2-6-4T No 42109.

RIGHT: Ivatt Class 2 2-6-2T No 41264 arrives at Thongs Bridge with a Holmfirth-Huddersfield-Bradford train just prior to closure in 1959.

BELOW: Fowler Class 4 2-6-4T No 42407 nears Berry Brow with a Clayton West-Huddersfield-Bradford local.

Gresley Class K3 2-6-0
No 61966 takes the Penistone
line as it climbs past Springwood
Junction after leaving
Huddersfield with a Sunday
Manchester-Marylebone express
diverted from the Woodhead
route due to engineering work.
There were numerous occasions
when GC trains were diverted
over this route in the early 1950s
while the Woodhead
electrification was being
completed. This required trains to
be reversed at Huddersfield.

UPPER LEFT: Converted 'Royal Scot' class three-cylinder 4-6-0 No 46124 *London Scottish* pulls away from Huddersfield with the 9am Liverpool Lime Street-Newcastle express.

LOWER LEFT: Aspinall LYR Class 2P 2-4-2T No 50757 waits to depart from Huddersfield with a Bradford Exchange local. These radial tanks were used on this service almost since first introduced.

BELOW: Stanier Class 5 2-6-0 No 42952 awaits the road out of Huddersfield with a Leeds Copley Hill-Liverpool freight.

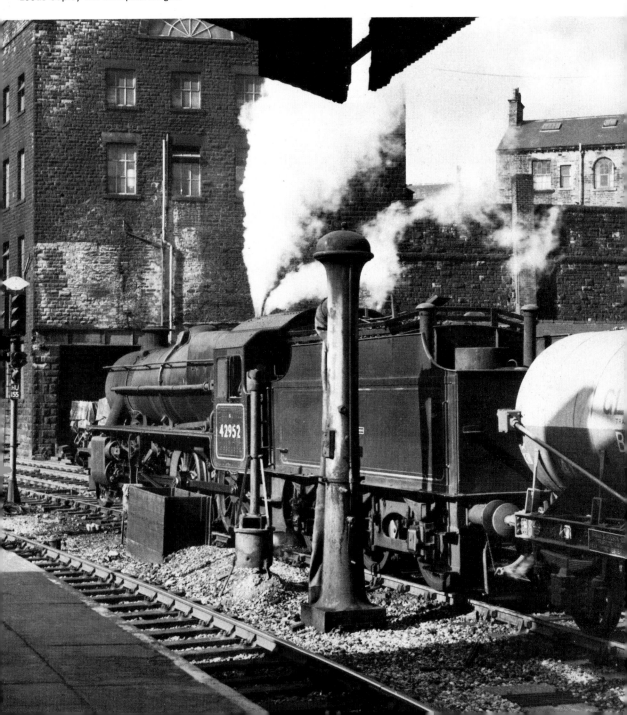

ABOVE: Stanier Class 8F 2-8-0 No 48602 climbs the 1 in 96 out of Huddersfield Tunnel past Springwood Junction with a Copley Hill-Liverpool freight in 1953.

UPPER RIGHT: Fowler 'Patriot' class 4-6-0 No 45518 *Bradshaw* leaves Gledholt Tunnel and passes Springwood Junction with a Liverpool Lime Street-Newcastle relief in July 1953.

LOWER RIGHT: The 9am Newcastle-Liverpool express comes out of Huddersfield Tunnel at Springwood Junction hauled by converted 'Royal Scot' 4-6-0 No 46152 *The King's Dragoon Guardsman* in October 1953.

LEFT: Stanier 'Black Five' 4-6-0 No 45312 passes Golcar with a Manchester-Scarborough holiday express.

BELOW: Fowler MR Class 2P 4-4-0 No 40552 pilots converted 'Royal Scot' 4-6-0 No 46124 *London Scottish* over the original 1849 half of Longwood Viaduct with the 9am Newcastle-Liverpool express.

RIGHT: Thompson Class B1 4-6-0 No 61176 and Stanier 'Jubilee' 4-6-0 No 45581 *Bihar and Orissa* climb towards Golcar with a Newcastle-Liverpool express on August 2, 1957.

BELOW RIGHT: 'Black Five' 4-6-0 No 45063 darkens the sky as it crosses from fast to slow lines at Gledholt Junction on the climb from Huddersfield with an evening Hull-Liverpool express.

ABOVE: Gresley Class K3 2-6-0 No 61883 climbs towards Marsden at Cellars Clough with a York-Ardwick freight in 1957. This train was re-routed via Leeds and Huddersfield at this time instead of using the normal Doncaster-Mexborough-Woodhead route.

LEFT: Another Class K3 Mogul, No 61966, passes the local permanent way gang as it clatters down through Longwood with a diverted Sunday Manchester London Road-Sheffield stopping train.

RIGHT: Thompson Class B1 4-6-0 No 61198 storms through Golcar with another diverted Sunday Sheffield-Manchester train, passing one of the LNWR skyscraper signals long since vanished.

ABOVE: Fowler LMS Class 7F 0-8-0 No 49509 climbs past Linthwaite Sidings with a Healey Mills-Diggle Junction freight in July 1951.

UPPER RIGHT: Another Fowler Class 7F 'Austin Seven', No 49618, heads downhill through Marsden with a Diggle Junction-Healey Mills train of coal empties in 1955.

LOWER RIGHT: A loaded coal train for Diggle Junction from Healey Mills trundles through Slaithwaite station behind Class 7F 0-8-0 No 49578 in July 1953.

LEFT: Twilight of steam in the Colne Valley with Riddles WD class 2-8-0 No 90351 pounding up the 1 in 112 through Linthwaite with a westbound haul of condemned wagons.

RIGHT: An unidentified Stanier Class 8F 2-8-0 blows off as it clanks down through Linthwaite with a Liverpool-Copley Hill freight.

ABOVE: The evening sun catches Thompson Class B1 4-6-0 No 61158 as it climbs through Linthwaite with a diverted Marylebone-Manchester express in 1953.

LEFT: Stanier 'Black Five' 4-6-0 No 45075 and 'Jubilee' 4-6-0 No 45600 *Bermuda* sweep across Slaithwaite Viaduct with an evening Liverpool-Newcastle express.

ABOVE: Caprotti 'Black Five' 4-6-0 No 44748 gets the right away from Slaithwaite with a Leeds-Blackpool excursion in July 1953.

LEFT: In original condition, Fowler 'Royal Scot' 4-6-0 No 46137 *The Prince of Wales' Volunteers (South Lancashire)* passes Slaithwaite with a Sunday Liverpool-Newcastle express.

UPPER RIGHT Another parallel boiler 'Scot', No 46158 *The Loyal Regiment,* hurries down through Linthwaite with the Sunday 9am Liverpool-Newcastle in May 1952.

LOWER RIGHT: Stanier 'Jubilee' 4-6-0 No 45558 *Manitoba* climbs towards Marsden with a Sunday York-Manchester train in 1952.

UPPER LEFT: Former Crosti-boilered BR standard Class 9F 2-10-0 No 92020 heads a Liverpool-Leeds freight downhill in the lee of Huck Hill, Marsden.

LOWER LEFT: Sunday at Slaithwaite with WD 2-8-0 No 90694 standing on an engineers train as a sister engine passes with similar train en route to Marsden.

ABOVE: A Stanier Class 4 2-6-4T coasts downhill from Marsden at Cellars Clough with an afternoon Manchester-Leeds slow train. Wessenden Moors are in the background.

RIGHT: A Sunday Stockport-Leeds parcels train heads away from Marsden behind Fowler Class 4 2-6-4T No 42412.

TOP: Rebuilt 'Patriot' class 4-6-0 No 45531 *Sir Frederick Harrison* rolls down the Colne Valley at Shaw Carr Bridge with the Sunday 9am Liverpool-Newcastle express.

ABOVE: Fowler LMS Class 2P 4-4-0 No 40581 has a final fling on express passenger work as it pilots Stanier 'Jubilee' 4-6-0 No 45581 *Bihar and Orissa* downhill from Marsden with a Liverpool-Newcastle express.

RIGHT: A Manchester-Leeds stopping train arrives at Marsden behind Fowler Class 4 2-6-4T No 42379 in March 1956. A 'Black Five' is heading away in the distance with a Manchester-bound stopping train.

ABOVE: LNWR Class 7F 0-8-0 No 49421 wheezes round the curve leading into Standege Tunnel at the summit of the climb from Huddersfield with a Copley Hill-Liverpool freight in June 1954.

UPPER RIGHT: The 9am Liverpool-Newcastle express swings round the curve out of Standege Tunnel behind Converted 'Royal Scot' class 4-6-0 No 46123 *Royal Irish Fusilier*.

LOWER RIGHT: Stanier 'Black Five' 4-6-0 No 45041 and rebuilt 'Patriot' 4-6-0 No 45534 *E. Tootal Broadhurst* negotiate the tortuous S bend from Marsden to Standedge Tunnel with a Newcastle-Liverpool express.

ABOVE: Stanier 'Black Five' 4-6-0 No 44896 emerges from the original 1849 bore of Standege Tunnel with an eastbound freight on June 4, 1966. The other single bore of this tunnel was built in 1870 while the double-track tunnel on the right was completed in 1894. The length of the original tunnel was 3 miles 64 yards.

UPPER LEFT: A high-level view of the approach to Standege Tunnel with a 'Black Five' on a Leeds-Manchester local neck-and-neck with 'Jubilee' 4-6-0 No 45621 Northern Rhodesia on a Leeds-Liverpool express routed via the Micklehurst loop. The Huddersfield and Ashton Canal boat repair warehouse and wharf are on the left.

LOWER LEFT: Fowler Class 4 2-6-4T No 42384 leaves the 1894 Standege Tunnel with a Stockport-Leeds parcels train in July 1954. The canal tunnel passed under the line here and entered the hillside between the 1894 and 1849 rail tunnels.

LNWR Class 7F 0-8-0 No 49343
approaches Diggle Junction with
a Liverpool-Leeds freight routed
via the Micklehurst loop.

RIGHT: Converted 'Royal Scot' class 4-6-0 No 46106 *Gordon Highlander,* fitted with BR standard type smoke deflectors, leaves Butterhouse Tunnel on the Micklehurst loop and approaches Diggle Junction with the 9am Liverpool-Newcastle express on Sunday June 26, 1960.

BELOW: Hughes/Fowler 'Crab' 2-6-0 No 42845 passes Diggle station with a Stockport-Bradford parcels train in 1960. Diggle water troughs were just inside Standege Tunnel and drained into the canal tunnel, which was at a slightly lower level.

LEFT: The 'Delph Donkey' push-and-pull train is propelled away from Measurements Halt by standard Class 2MT 2-6-2T No 84012 on its journey down to Greenfield Junction and eventually Oldham in August 1954. Measurements Halt was opened during World War II when the Oldham-based firm of Orme's moved out to avoid the air raids. The Delph branch closed to passenger traffic in May 1955.

RIGHT: Evening light catches 'Black Five' 4-6-0 No 44870 and 'Patriot' 4-6-0 No 45515 Caernarvon riding high over the Huddersfield and Ashton Canal as they cross Saddleworth Viaduct with the 5pm Liverpool Lime Street-Newcastle express in September 1956.

BELOW: A pigeon special from Sunderland to Southampton crosses Saddleworth Viaduct behind 'Crab' 2-6-0 No 42859 and BR standard Class 5MT 4-6-0 No 73014 on August 28, 1954. Below the viaduct to the left the canal can be seen crossing the River Tame — source of the Mersey.

BOTTOM: Fowler Class 4 2-6-4T No 42354 sets out across the viaduct from Saddleworth station with an evening Leeds-Stockport stopping train.

ABOVE: Stanier Class 4 2-6-4T No 42572 with a teatime Manchester-Leeds local passes the massive cooling towers of Stalybridge Power Station at Black Rock.

UPPER LEFT: An LNWR Class 7F 0-8-0 trundles down through Uppermill on the Micklehurst loop with a Leeds Copley Hill-Liverpool freight on a September evening in 1956.

LEFT: A 'Black Five' 4-6-0 makes a smokey exit from Stalybridge with the 12.55 Manchester Exchange-Leeds City stopping train as a Leeds-Blackpool train heads through the station, having come off the Micklehurst loop.

ABOVE: Mill chimneys dominate this view of standard Class 5MT 4-6-0 No 73095 leaving Stalybridge on a dull day with a Manchester-Leeds local.

LEFT: A Saturday Leeds-Liverpool express enters Stalybridge behind rebuilt 'Patriot' 4-6-0 No 45531 *Sir Frederick Harrison*. The train is formed of Bain MR low-roofed suburban stock.

BELOW: Stanier 'Black Five' and 'Jubilee' 4-6-0s Nos 45080 and 45646 *Napier* sweep round the curve through Miles Platting station after climbing Miles Platting bank out of Manchester with the 9am Liverpool-Newcastle express.

BOTTOM: With wagon brakes pinned down Robinson ROD Class O4/3 2-8-0 No 63846 cautiously descends the 1 in 47 of Miles Platting bank into Manchester Victoria Station with a cross-Manchester freight from Ardwick to Ordsall Lane.

LEFT: 'Jubilee' 4-6-0 No 45600 *Bermuda* approaches Manchester Exchange with a summer Llandudno-Leeds express.

RIGHT: Rebuilt 'Patriot' 4-6-0 No 45525 *Colwn Bay* departs from Manchester Exchange with the 9 am Newcastle-Liverpool express. A Class 2P 4-4-0 used for banking trains up Miles Platting bank stands on the left.

BELOW: Engine numbers are carefully noted as a WD 2-8-0 passes through Manchester Victoria with the Newton Heath breakdown train. Aspinall LYR Class 3F 0-6-0 No 52328 waits to bank a freight train up Miles Platting bank.

ABOVE: A Holyhead 'Royal Scot' 4-6-0, No 46151 *The Royal Horse Guardsman*, waits to leave Manchester Exchange with an express for Liverpool Lime Street in 1955.

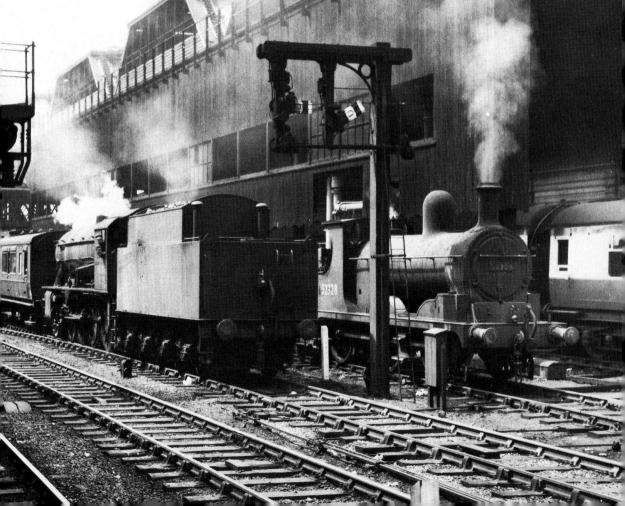

LEFT: 'Jubilee' 4-6-0 No 45581 *Bihar and Orissa* crosses from the through road to the platform in Manchester Exchange with the 9am Hull-Liverpool express.

BELOW: Standard Class 5MT 4-6-0 No 73137, fitted with Caprotti valve gear, hits the bottom of Miles Platting bank in Manchester Victoria with a westbound freight. Aspinall 0-6-0 No 52275 awaits its next banking duty.

UPPER RIGHT: A Manchester Victoria-Rochdale-Oldham Mumps-Manchester Victoria circular local departs from Rochdale on a wet afternoon behind Stanier Class 4 2-6-4T No 42545.

LOWER RIGHT: Aspinall Class 3F 0-6-0 No 52317 is seen from the platform of Oldham Clegg Street as it passes through Oldham Central with a freight from Werneth for the Rochdale line.

ABOVE: On the LYR Calder Valley main line Stanier 'Black Five' 4-6-0 No 44690 canters up the gradient from Littleborough to Summit Tunnel with a Liverpool Exchange-Bradford Exchange express.

LEFT: Hughes/Fowler 'Crab' 2-6-0 No 42842 accelerates past Summit Tunnel West signalbox as it leaves the short Rochdale Road Tunnel with a Bradford-Manchester express. A flight of locks on the Rochdale Canal can be seen above the engine.

RIGHT: Riddles WD 2-8-0 No 90687 is glimpsed on a wet day in the short gap between Summit and Rochdale Road Tunnels with a train of Yorkshire coal for Lancashire.

Rain clouds are brewing over the Pennines as WD 2-8-0 No 90245 blasts its way uphill out of the Calder Valley at Summit Tunnel East signalbox with a Healey Mills-Manchester freight train.

ABOVE: The solitary 'Black Five' 4-6-0 fitted with Stephenson's outside link motion, No 44767, emerges from Winterbutlee Tunnel near Walsden on the climb from Todmorden to Summit Tunnel with a York-Manchester express.

UPPER RIGHT: A Manchester-Bradford stopping train nears Stansfield Hall as it heads away from Todmorden behind 'Black Five' No 44912.

LOWER RIGHT: 'Black Five' 4-6-0 No 44695 coasts downhill towards Todmorden and crosses the original 1840 turreted bridge over the Rochdale Canal with a Liverpool-Leeds express. The deck girders of this bridge were replaced by the LMS during World War II.

RIGHT: Amid typical Yorkshire/Lancashire border scenery Hughes/Fowler 'Crab' 2-6-0 No 42864 crosses the 18-arch Gauxholme Viaduct as it leaves Todmorden on the climb to Summit Tunnel with a Burnley-Manchester local in the mid-1950s.

BELOW: Grimy 'Black Five' 4-6-0 No 44987 pounds through Todmorden station with a York-Manchester express.

LEFT: Class 8F 2-8-0 No 48152 comes clanking downhill into Todmorden with coal empties for Healey Mills on a spring evening.

RIGHT: At Stansfield Hall WD 2-8-0 No 90548 awaits the call to bank a westbound freight out of the Calder Valley to Copy Pit summit on the line to Burnley.

UPPER LEFT: 'Jubilee' 4-6-0
No 45647 *Sturdee* passes Dover
Bridge Siding, west of Hebden
Bridge, with the 8.37am Leeds
City-Blackpool train on June 4,
1966.

LOWER LEFT: The Stephenson
valve gear 'Black Five',
No 44767, passes Hebden
Bridge with a Liverpool
Exchange-Leeds Central express.

ABOVE: Sowerby Bridge Station
on April 11, 1955 with Aspinall
LYR Class 2P 2-4-2T No 50818
on station pilot duty and a
Fairburn Class 4 2-6-4T pulling
out light.

RIGHT: Another Aspinall radial
tank at Sowerby Bridge:
No 50865 replenishes its water
supply after arrival with a local
from Wakefield.

ABOVE: Aspinall Class 3F 0-6-0 No 52515 staggers past Mirfield with a coal train from Castleford for Lancashire via the Calder Valley

LEFT: A Huddersfield-Wakefield local passes Spen Valley Junction behind Aspinall Class 2P 2-4-2T No 50762.

UPPER RIGHT: Class 9F 2-10-0 No 92058 brings a summer Saturday Blackpool-Wakefield-Castleford holiday train past Heaton Lodge Junction, meeting point of the LNWR and LYR trans-Pennine routes.

LOWER RIGHT: With steam to spare Stanier Class 3 2-6-2T No 40075 drifts past Heaton Lodge Junction with a teatime Wakefield Kirkgate-Sowerby Bridge local. The Leeds New Line can be seen climbing away behind the train.

LEFT: In the shadow of Thornhill Power Station Fowler Class 7F 0-8-0 No 49578 crosses over from the LNWR Leeds line to the LYR main line at Thornhill LNW Junction with a lightweight freight from Copley Hill to Healey Mills. The engine will have to run round its train before continuing its journey.

TOP: Thompson Class B1 4-6-0 No 61320 passes under the LNWR Thornhill-Leeds line as it approaches Thornhill station with a diverted Leeds Central-Kings Cross express.

ABOVE: An unscheduled express freight, probably perishables from Goole to Manchester, passes Ravensthorpe & Thornhill station behind 'Jubilee' 4-6-0 No 45729 *Furious* of Carlisle Kingmoor shed.

LEFT: Fowler Class 4 2-6-4T No 42312 approaches Lady Anne Crossing, Batley soon after leaving Morley Tunnel with a Leeds-Huddersfield stopping train on July 6, 1957.

BELOW: Fowler Class 2P 4-4-0 No 40690 pilots a 'Black Five' 4-6-0 on a Liverpool-Hull express seen coming off Union Mill Viaduct at the approach to Batley station.

UPPER RIGHT: A Newcastle-Liverpool express leaves the western end of Morley Tunnel hauled by 'Black Five' 4-6-0 No 44934 and converted 'Royal Soct' 4-6-0 No 46152 *The King's Dragoon Guardsman*.

LOWER RIGHT: Stanier 'Jubilee' 4-6-0 No 45708 *Resolution* swings round the curve from Morley station and tunnel en route for Leeds on July 6, 1957 with the 11am Liverpool-Hull express.

LEFT: Gresley LNER Class J39 0-6-0 No 64754 climbs into Batley GNR station beside the LNWR Union Mill Viaduct with through coaches from Kings Cross to Bradford taken over at Wakefield.

LOWER LEFT: The 11am Liverpool-Hull express crosses Union Mill Viaduct into Batley with converted 'Royal Scot' No 46123 *Royal Irish Fusilier* in charge.

BELOW: Gresley GNR Class J50 0-6-0T No 68901 climbs into Batley with a pick-up freight from Wrenthorpe. Note the elevated GNR signalbox above the left-hand side of the station giving clear views for miles around.

BOTTOM: Stanier Class 5 2-6-0 No 42952 pulls away from the LNWR platform at Batley with a summer Saturday Leeds-North Wales train.

LEFT: Conference time at Farnley Junction motive power depot before moving off with Riddles WD 2-8-0 No 90322 after coaling.

RIGHT: Fowler Class 4F 0-6-0 No 44235 pilots 'Black Five' 4-6-0 No 45294 past Farnley Junction with a Copley Hill-Manchester empty stock train.

BELOW: A Llandudno-Leeds express comes off the Leeds New Line from Spen Valley Junction at Farnley Junction behind 'Black Five' 4-6-0 No 45095.

ABOVE: Stanier Class 8F 2-8-0 No 48626 wheels a cross-Leeds tanker train through Leeds City to Neville Hill in July 1956.

LEFT: Converted 'Royal Scot' 4-6-0 No 46106 *Gordon Highlander* backs through Leeds City after handing over the 9am Liverpool-Newcastle express to an NER Pacific.

RIGHT: Gresley LNER Class V2 three-cylinder 2-6-2 No 60938 of March shed waits to back out of Leeds City after arrival with a summer Saturday train from Scarborough and Filey.

Gresley LNER 'Hunt' Class D49/2
three-cylinder 4-4-0 No 62726
The Meynell departs from Leeds
City (formerly the NER New
Station) with an express for Hull.
This engine was the first member
of Gresley's 'Hunt' Class fitted
with Lentz rotary-cam poppet
valve gear and was originally
named *Leicestershire*. These
engines put in yeomen service on
the lines radiating north and east
from Leeds from the early 1930s
until replaced by diesel multiple-
units.

LEFT: Ivatt LMS-type Class 4 2-6-0 No 43052 heads a Leeds-York stopping train away from Marsh Lane station.

RIGHT: Class A8 4-6-2T No 69882 eases off the relief line through Marsh Lane Cutting with empty stock from Neville Hill for Leeds City. This engine was built by Raven of the NER as a 4-4-4T and was subsequently rebuilt as a 4-6-2T by Gresley.

ABOVE: One of the famous Worsdell NER R Class 4-4-0s, now Class D20 No 62372, potters home light to Neville Hill passing through the massive Marsh Lane Cutting which was originally a twin-line tunnel opened out in 1892-4.

LEFT: Gresley Class A3 Pacific No 60082 *Neil Gow* approaches Leeds City over Marsh Lane Viaduct with the 9am Newcastle-Liverpool express, soon to hand over its train to a pair of LMR Class 7P 4-6-0s for the climb over Standedge.

LEFT: Gresley Class J39 0-6-0 No 64863 arrives at Wetherby with a Whit Monday race special from Doncaster via Leeds.

LOWER LEFT: BR standard Class 4MT 2-6-4T No 80118 approaches Arthington as it comes round the curve from Bramhope Tunnel with a Leeds-Harrogate-Ripon express.

RIGHT: Thompson Class B1 4-6-0 No 61353 climbs the 1 in 100 past Horsforth to Bramhope Tunnel with a summer Saturday through train from Kings Cross to Ripon.

BELOW: The southbound 'Queen of Scots' Pullman draws sedately to a halt at Harrogate behind Gresley Class A3 Pacific No 60074 Harvester.

LEFT: Fowler LMS Class 4P three-cylinder compound 4-4-0 No 41063 struggles away from Skipton with a 10 coach holiday Saturday Morecambe-Leeds express.

BELOW: Stanier 'Black Five' 4-6-0 No 44901 passes under the Yorkshire Dales branch as it approaches Skipton with a Bradford-Morecambe stopping train.

ABOVE: With its snifting valves chattering, Fowler MR Class 4F 0-6-0 No 43916 drifts down to Skipton with a pick-up freight from the Embsay branch. It is crossing the bridge featured in the picture on the left.

UPPER LEFT: Stanier Class 3 2-6-2T No 40139 accelerates away from Keighley with a Bradford-Skipton local.

LOWER LEFT: A Skipton-Stourton freight passes through Keighley station hauled by rebuilt Johnson MR Class 3F 0-6-0 No 43257.

RIGHT: Ivatt Class 2 2-6-0 No 46442 leaves Shipley with a Bradford Forster Square-Skipton local. This station has always been a problem with no platform on the main line. The local service from Leeds to Skipton had to be run in two parts to Bradford, with cross-platform interchange at Shipley if you were lucky.

BELOW: Hughes/Fowler 'Crab' 2-6-0 No 42851 is grateful for an application of sand to greasy rails as it restarts from a signal stop on Shipley Curve with a Morecambe train during a heavy shower.

BELOW: Well-groomed Holbeck 'Royal Scot' 4-6-0 No 46108 *Seaforth Highlander* grinds round the curve from Leeds City to Whitehall Junction with the down 'Thames-Clyde Express'.

BOTTOM: Fowler Class 4P compound 4-4-0 No 41087 brings a two-coach Bradford Forster Square-Leeds City local round Holbeck triangle.

RIGHT: Another Bradford local departs from Leeds City (the former MR Wellington side) headed by Fowler Compound 4-4-0 No 41196. The leading vans carry North Sea fish for Bradford Market, transferred from the NER side of the station.

LOWER RIGHT: BR standard 'Clan' Class 6MT Pacific No 72009 *Clan Stewart* brings empty stock from Armley to Leeds City past Wellington Junction while filling in on a summer Saturday after working in from Carlisle.

UPPER LEFT: The first Ivatt GNR Class J6 0-6-0, No 64170, pulls out of the GNR side of Bradford Exchange with empty stock of an arrival from Kings Cross before setting back into another platform for departure. The LYR signalbox is next to the train.

LOWER LEFT: Fairburn Class 4 2-6-4T No 42108 climbs the 1 in 50 out of Bradford Exchange to Bowling Junction past Coal Shoots signalbox with a local for Low Moor. The derelict GNR St Dunstans Station is on the right with the line to Halifax/Keighley passing under the 2-6-4T.

ABOVE: Ivatt GNR Class N1 0-6-2T No 69474 leaves Laisterdyke in evening light with the Bradford portion of a Kings Cross-Leeds express taken over at Wakefield. The line on the right leads to Bowling Junction.

LEFT: Thompson Class B1 4-6-0 No 61110 crosses the ceiling of Yorkshire as it blasts uphill through Morley Top on the climb to Cutlers Junction and Bradford with the through portion from Wakefield of an express from Kings Cross.

BELOW: In the opposite direction Ivatt Class J6 0-6-0 No 64170 comes clattering down through Morley Top with the Bradford portion of an express for Kings Cross. The tunnel vent of the LNWR Morley Tunnel can be seen above the signalbox.

UPPER RIGHT: Gresley Class J50 0-6-0T No 68901 blasts out of Wakefield Road Tunnel, Dewsbury with the daily pick-up freight from Batley to Wrenthorpe Yard.

LOWER RIGHT: A Wakefield-Bradford local departs from Dewsbury Central behind Ivatt Class N1 0-6-2T No 69440.

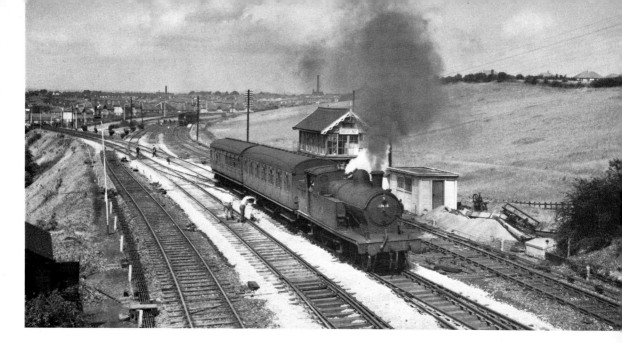

UPPER LEFT: Gresley Class V2 2-6-2 No 60820 rounds the curve past Copley Hill motive power depot with a Leeds Central-Kings Cross express.

LEFT: Smoke pours from Gresley Class A3 Pacific No 60046 *Diamond Jubilee* as it passes Copley Hill with the up 'White Rose.'

TOP: Robinson GCR Class C13 4-4-2T No 67438 climbs the 1 in 100 through Beeston Junction with a Leeds Central-Wakefield local. This was one of a handful of these tanks shedded at Ardsley for service in the West Riding.

ABOVE: Another Atlantic tank in the shape of Ivatt GNR Class C12 No 67372 at Copley Hill shed. They were used for many years on the GNR lines in the West Riding, but faded away in the early 1950s.

121

ABOVE: Robinson Class 04/7 2-8-0 No 63588 battles uphill towards Lofthouse East Junction near Outwood on the joint GNR, LYR and NER Methley branch with a heavy coal drag from Castleford to Doncaster via Wakefield Westgate.

UPPER RIGHT: Another haul of coal comes off the Methley branch, passing through the closed Lofthouse & Outwood station behind Thompson Class B1 4-6-0 No 61310.

LOWER RIGHT: Gresley Class J39 0-6-0 No 64796 swings round the curve through Dudley Hill station with coal empties from Bradford to Wakefield on a September evening.